Freaky Fish

Pufferfish

Tori Miller

PowerKiDS press™

New York

Published in 2009 by The Rosen Publishing Group, Inc.
29 East 21st Street, New York, NY 10010

First Edition

Editor: Joanne Randolph
Book Design: Greg Tucker
Photo Researcher: Jessica Gerweck

Photo Credits: Cover, pp. 5, 9 © Robert Wu/Getty Images; pp. 7, 11 Shutterstock.com; pp. 12–13 © Kelvin Aitken/Age Fotostock: p. 15 © Jeff Rotman/Getty Images; p. 17 © Juniors Bildarchiv/Age Fotostock; p. 19 © David Hall/Getty Images; p. 21 © Chris Newbert/Getty Images.

Library of Congress Cataloging-in-Publication Data

Miller, Tori.
    Pufferfish / Tori Miller. — 1st ed.
        p. cm. — (Freaky fish)
    Includes index.
    ISBN 978-1-4358-2818-6 (library binding) — ISBN 978-1-4358-3171-1 (pbk.)
ISBN 978-1-4358-3177-3 (6-pack)
    1. Puffers (Fish)—Juvenile literature. I. Title.
    QL638.T32M55 2009
    597'.64—dc22
                                                            2008030654

Manufactured in the United States of America

Contents

Underwater Balloons

A hungry shark is looking for something to eat. It sees a little fish swimming near a **coral reef**. The shark swims closer. It opens its mouth to eat the fish, but something has happened! The little fish is not little anymore. Now it is a big, round fish with **spikes** sticking out all over its body. It is a pufferfish! The shark swims away to find its dinner somewhere else.

A pufferfish is a bit like an underwater balloon! When in danger, the pufferfish swells up to many times its usual size. The pufferfish fools its **predators** into thinking it is a fish that is much too big to eat.

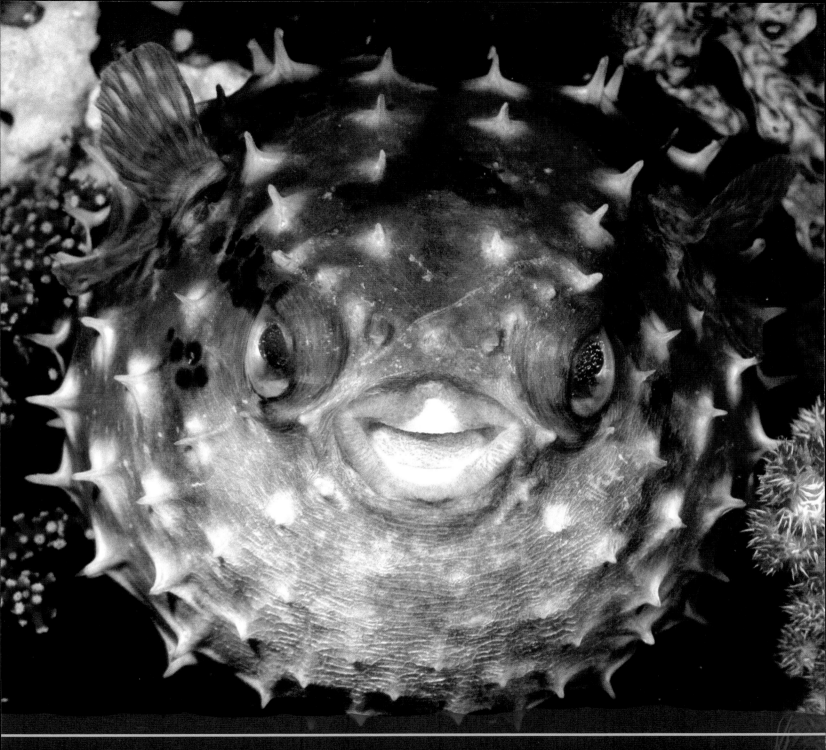

This is a kind of pufferfish called a porcupine fish. It gets its name because it has pointy spikes, like a porcupine, that stick out when it puffs up.

Puffer Looks

When pufferfish are not puffed up, they are club shaped with big heads and big eyes. Pufferfish have tough, or strong, skin. Most pufferfish are dark so they can hide in their **environment**. Some are brightly colored. Pufferfish can also have spots or other markings.

Pufferfish have several fins, but they cannot swim fast. They can swim forward and backward, though!

Some pufferfish are very small. The smallest is just 1 inch (2.5 cm) long. The biggest pufferfish are more than 3 feet (1 m) long. Of course, they all get much bigger when they puff up!

Here you can see the club shape of this pufferfish. It has small spikes that come from each of the dark spots on its body.

Puffing Up!

There are more than 120 **species**, or kinds, of pufferfish. Some of the pufferfish species include the white-spotted puffer, the green puffer, and the longnose puffer, to name just a few. All of them can puff themselves up to several times their usual size. This is why pufferfish are sometimes called balloonfish, swellfish, or blowfish.

Pufferfish puff up by quickly swallowing large amounts of water. A pufferfish that is just 8 inches (20 cm) long can hold as much as 1 quart (1 l) of water! When a pufferfish is puffed up, it becomes very rigid, or hard to bend. This makes it hard for predators to get their mouths around a puffed-up puffer!

This is a white-spotted puffer, also called a guinea fowl or golden pufferfish, that has puffed itself up. When it is not puffed up, this fish can be up to 19 inches (48 cm) long.

Where Do Pufferfish Live?

Pufferfish can be found in the Atlantic Ocean, the Pacific Ocean, and the Indian Ocean. Some kinds of pufferfish swim into places where the freshwater from rivers mixes with the salt water of the sea. They may even swim up the rivers to live in freshwater. Some kinds of pufferfish live only in freshwater.

Pufferfish like shallow water, or water that is not deep. They often spend their time near coral reefs and rocks or near the bottom of the sea. This means that adult pufferfish are more likely to be found near the land than out in the open sea.

Porcupine fish live in coral reefs in the warm waters of the Atlantic Ocean, Pacific Ocean, and Indian Ocean. You can see the spikes on this porcupine fish's skin in this photo.

The Pufferfish: Freaky Facts

- Pufferfish do not have scales, or the plates that make up the skin of some fish.

- Pufferfish can close their eyes. Most fish cannot do this.

- If a pufferfish feels **threatened** when it is not in the water, it will use air to puff up instead of water.

- Baby pufferfish can puff up almost from the time they are born.

- Baby pufferfish have thin shells for the first 10 days of their lives.

- The smallest pufferfish are called dwarf pufferfish.

- About 50 people each year die from eating pufferfish.

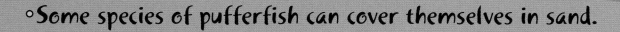

○Some species of pufferfish can cover themselves in sand.

○People have found dead barracudas with pufferfish trapped in their throats.

○There is a pufferfish named Bloat in the movie *Finding Nemo.*

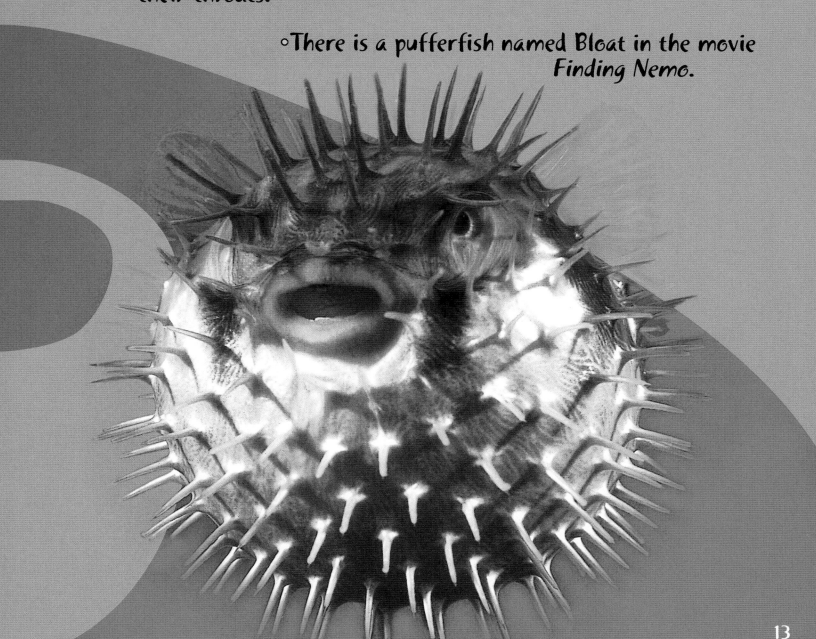

What's for Dinner?

Most pufferfish eat **algae** and small **invertebrates** such as worms, squid, and sea snails. Larger species eat clams, mussels, crayfish, shrimp, and other shellfish.

The mouth of a pufferfish looks a lot like the beak, or bill, of a parrot. This beak is made up of three or four **fused** teeth, which pufferfish use to eat their food. They can use their beaklike mouths to cut through a piece of coral. Then they eat the living parts of the coral and leave the rest. Pufferfish can also use their mouths to break open the shells of clams and crabs.

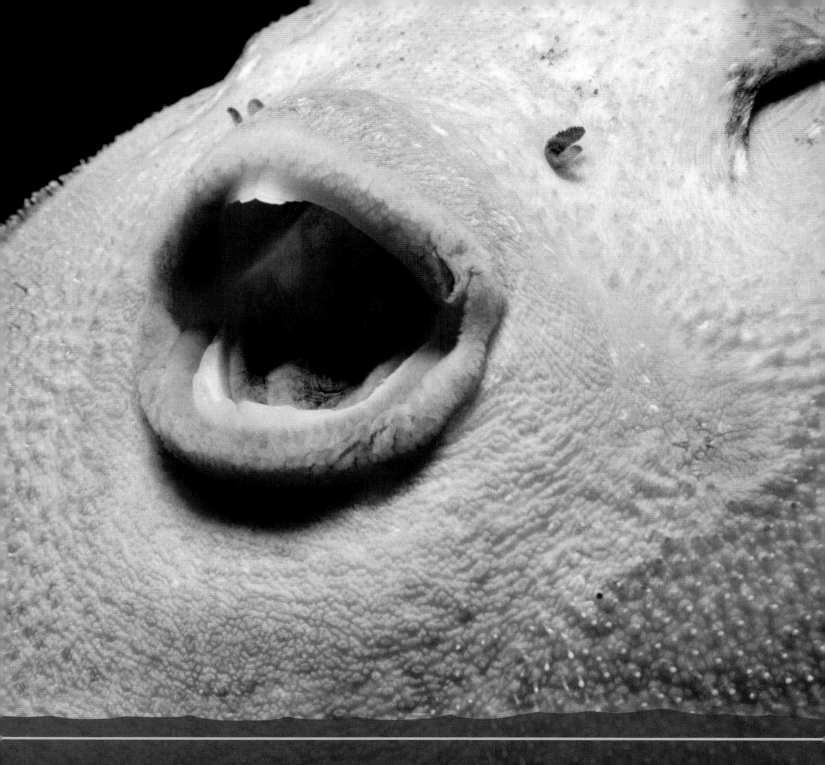

This is a close-up look at a puffer's mouth and teeth. As you can see, its teeth are all one piece.

Watch Out, Puffer!

Barracudas, sea snakes, and sharks may eat baby puffers. Adult pufferfish do not get eaten very often because when they puff up, they become too big to swallow. Also, some kinds of pufferfish have spines, or thin, sharp parts like needles. The spines stick straight out when the pufferfish is puffed out.

Scientists believe that pufferfish need their special talent because they are too slow to swim away from predators. Most predators do not want to try to eat a big, rigid ball, though. They will move on to easier prey. This is lucky, since when puffers puff up, they swim twice as slow as they generally do!

Here a reef lizardfish is eating a pufferfish. Lizardfish do not seem to be bothered by pufferfish spines or their puffed-up shape.

Poisonous Puffers

If a predator somehow swallows a pufferfish before it puffs up, it may still be in for a nasty surprise. Most pufferfish are **poisonous**. The poison inside a pufferfish is called tetrodotoxin. It is one of the strongest poisons in nature. Like many other poisonous animals, poisonous pufferfish are brightly colored. The bright colors tell predators not to eat them.

The poison inside the pufferfish will make it taste bad to most predators. It can also kill the predator. However, some fish, such as the tiger shark, are not hurt by the pufferfish's poison.

This puffer is colored bright yellow to let other animals know it does not taste very good. If a fish tries to take a bite anyway, the puffer will puff itself up.

Puffer Babies

Pufferfish lay eggs in the open water. The eggs float in the water and hatch, or open, in about 4 days. Newly hatched pufferfish are called **larvae**. They are about ¼ inch (6 mm) long. Larvae are yellow with red spots.

After three weeks, the larvae change into **juvenile** pufferfish. They grow fins and teeth. They also get dark spots on the undersides of their bodies. The spots help the young pufferfish blend in with seaweed in the ocean. Juveniles stay in the open water until they grow into adult pufferfish. Then they move to shallow water near shore.

This is a juvenile starry pufferfish. It will grow to be around 4 feet (1.2 m) long and will turn white with black spots as it gets older and larger.

Pufferfish and People

The poison in pufferfish is a great danger to people. There is enough poison in one pufferfish to kill 30 people! However, some people eat pufferfish anyway. In Japan, specially trained cooks prepare a dish called **fugu**. Fugu costs a lot of money. The cook must know exactly which parts of the pufferfish are safe to eat and how to prepare them.

It is much safer to look at pufferfish than to eat them! You can find pufferfish at many public aquariums. Some people keep them in small home aquariums as well. Maybe someday you will see a pufferfish!

Glossary

algae (AL-jee) Plantlike living things without roots or stems that live in water.

coral reef (KOR-ul REEF) An underwater hill of coral, or hard matter made up of the bones of tiny sea animals.

environment (en-VY-ern-ment) All the living things and conditions of a place.

fugu (FYOO-goo) A Japanese dish made with pufferfish.

fused (FYOOZD) Joined together.

invertebrates (in-VER-teh-brets) Animals without backbones, or bones along the back of an animal.

juvenile (JOO-vuh-nyl) An animal that is nearly grown but not yet an adult.

larvae (LAHR-vee) Insects or fish in the early life stage in which they have a wormlike form.

poisonous (POYZ-nus) Causing pain or death.

predators (PREH-duh-terz) Animals that kill other animals for food.

species (SPEE-sheez) One kind of living thing. All people are one species.

spikes (SPYKS) Sharp, pointy things shaped like a spear or a needle.

threatened (THREH-tund) Acted like something could cause hurt.

Index

Web Sites

Due to the changing nature of Internet links, PowerKids Press has developed an online list of Web sites related to the subject of this book. This site is updated regularly. Please use this link to access the list:

www.powerkidslinks.com/ffish/puffers/